Silly Stories

HOUGHTON MIFFLIN

BOSTON • MORRIS PLAINS, NJ

California • Colorado • Georgia • Illinois • New Jersey • Texas

Design, Art Management, and Page Production: Silver Editions.

Contents

Len and Linda's Picnic

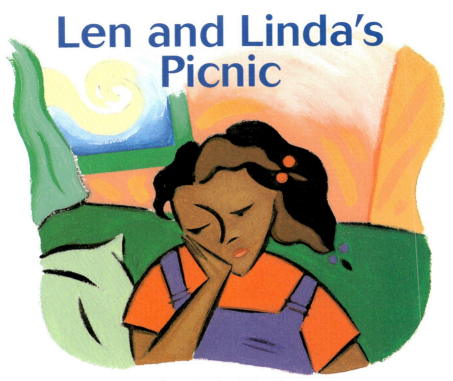

by Becky Ward
illustrated by Jill Benasheck

Linda sat with her chin in her hand.

"I can't think of a game to play," she said sadly.

Ring, ring, ring, went the bell. Ring, ring, ring.

"Someone has come to visit," thought Linda.

Linda went to her front door.

"My best pal Len! I am glad you came to visit. I need a game to play," said Linda.

"You are in luck," said Len. "I just bought a new ball. We can roll it and catch it. It will be fun."

Just then, big drops of rain started falling.

"We can't play outside when it is raining," said Linda. "This is a sad, sad day."

Len sat down on the steps to think. Soon he said, "I know just what we need to make this sad day fun!"

big basket
cloth
plates
napkins
plastic cups
tea · jam
toast

Len went to the kitchen. He got a
pad and a pen and made this list.

Len found the things on his list. Linda
packed them in the big basket. Len took
the basket and left.

Linda looked at the rain on the
window. "This wet day is no fun. We
can't picnic until it stops raining."

5

"Linda," yelled Len. "Come see. You will think this game is fun."

Linda looked and looked until she found Len in the den.

"Look at this! It's an indoor picnic!" said Len.

Linda jumped up and down with glee.

6

Drip, drip, drip went the rain. Drip, drip, drip. But Len and Linda's picnic did not get wet.

An Ice Cream Crash

by Becky Ward
illustrated by S. Signorino

Will and Jill were feeling hungry.
The twins looked in the kitchen. Jill
looked high. Will looked low. Then
Will and Jill looked at each other.
"No ice cream," said Jill.

"We can ride to town and get ice cream," said Will.

"Let's get going," said Jill.

Will and Jill jumped on their bike and started down the steep hill to Bob's Food Store in town.

10

Down, down, down the hill they
rolled. Zoom! Zoom! Zoom! They could
not stop. Until . . . bump, crash, boom.
Their trip ended fast.

"We bumped into a truck," said Will.
"And we bumped it hard," added Jill.
"Help us, please!" yelled the twins.

Sam rushed from his truck. "What is this?" he asked.

"We went looking for ice cream and rolled down that hill fast. We bumped into this truck," said Jill.

"My knee is scratched," said Will, starting to cry.

"Too bad," said Sam, as he helped Will
and Jill get up. "Maybe this will make
you feel better."

Sam reached into the back of his truck
and handed each twin an ice cream
cone.

Sam took the twins home.

"Crashing into an ice cream truck is not fun," said Will.

"But eating ice cream IS!" added Jill.

15

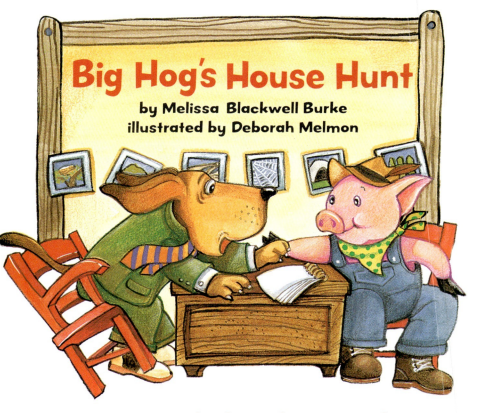

Big Hog's House Hunt

by Melissa Blackwell Burke

illustrated by Deborah Melmon

Big Hog was looking for a new home when he met Hot Dog.

"It's my job to help pals look for new homes," said Hot Dog. "It just so happens that at the present time, I have seven homes for sale. I bet I can sell you a home!"

"Let's hop on it," said Big Hog.

Big Hog and Hot Dog set off on a
house hunt. Hot Dog led Big Hog to a
grand web.

"It's a special web, near the bus stop
and the vet. It's extra big. Do you like
it a lot or not, Big Hog?"

"No," said Big Hog. "A web is not a
good home for a hog. A web gets too
much sun, and it's not big enough."

"Not a problem," said Hot Dog. "We'll
keep on looking."

"Let's hop on it," said Big Hog.

Big Hog and Hot Dog went down the road. Hot Dog led Big Hog to a cub's den.

"It's a fine den. It is dark, and it is extra, extra big. It will make a good home for you. Do you like it a lot or not, Big Hog?"

"No," said Big Hog. "A den might be good for a cub, but it's not the right home for me. A den does not get enough sun, and it is much too big."

"Not a problem," said Hot Dog. "We'll keep on looking."

"Let's hop on it," said Big Hog.

But Hot Dog and Big Hog did not set off.

"Let me think," said Hot Dog. "Not a web. Not a den. We'll keep on looking. We can see five more homes. I will not give up yet."

All of a sudden, Big Hog hopped up. "Such fun! You brought me here for a reason, Hot Dog."

"Yes! Yes!" said Hot Dog. "Surprise! This is a special pen. It has lots of mud and lots of space. Do you like it a lot or not, Big Hog?"

"Yes! I will take it," said Big Hog. "It is just right. Welcome to my new home, Hot Dog! Visit me any time."

He hugged Hot Dog. "Good job," said Big Hog. "You found the right home for me."

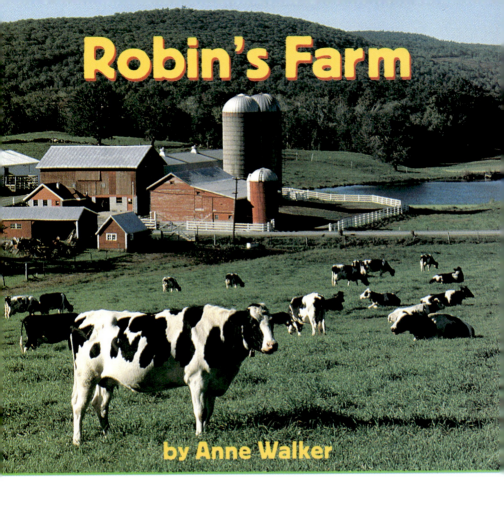

Robin's Farm

by Anne Walker

Many animals live on Robin's farm
in New York.

Cows graze on green grass. Late
in the day the cows go inside for
milking.

Robin's cat is named Jazz. It has striped fur with a big white spot. It takes naps in a basket.

At night Jazz catches mice in the barn.

26

Robin's white rabbit hops about in
a large rabbit hutch.

The rabbit's pink ears stand up
when Robin brings food.

Robin's dog Flash rides in Robin's old red pickup truck.

Flash sticks his head out the window. They ride to the feed store to get feed for Robin's horses.

A hen sat on three brown eggs in
the hen house.

Now three new chicks will play with
Flash.

Robin had a special surprise this
spring. Her pig Agnes gave birth to
six piglets. Agnes takes good care of
her six brand new babies.

The pigs stay warm at night. They sleep in the barn with Agnes.

Robin closes the barn door, and then she smiles.

"Good night, new pals. Good night, Agnes."

Jane's Mistake

by Patty Moynahan
illustrated by Marsha Winborn

Jane Crane has a nice smile, but Jane is not wearing a smile now. Her bracelet is missing.

Did someone take Jane's bracelet?

33

"I made my bracelet," said Jane. "It has a bead for each letter in my name. Who might take my bracelet with JANE CRANE on it? Whoever took it might switch the letters and spell a different name — like ACE RENNA or ENJAN RACE!"

"Look!" shouted Jake. "Kate has a bead bracelet. It might be your bracelet, Jane. Let's ask her if it is. Quick! We must move fast."

The kids began to chase Kate.

"I think that's my bracelet!"
yelled Jane.

Kate looked at them. Then she
went inside the gym.

"Don't try to hide!" yelled Jane.

Kate stopped. Jane and her
friends also stopped.
"This bracelet is mine," said Kate.
She held out her arm.

Jane read each word on Kate's
bracelet.

The beads did not spell JANE
CRANE. They spelled ALWAYS
BE KIND.

Jane's face turned red.

"You poor thing!" said Jane.

Just then Miss Fine came in. She had found Jane's bracelet on a hall floor.

"Thanks," said Jane. Then Jane looked at Kate. "From now on, I will try to be more kind."

Kate gave Jane a big smile.

The Big Surprise

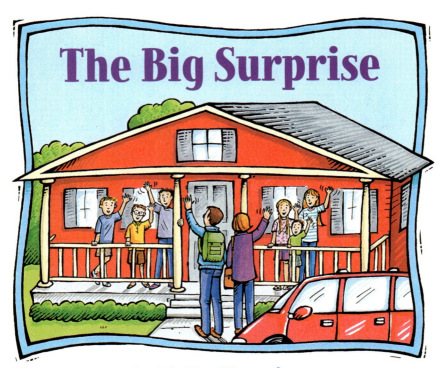

by Patty Moynahan
illustrated by Ruth Flanigan

Mom and Pop Lane live in a big red
house. Six Lane children live in the big
red house, too.

One fine day, Mom and Pop went on
a trip.

"See you soon!" said Mom and Pop.

"Have fun, Mom and Pop!"

"Let's surprise Mom and Pop," said
Big Sis. "We can clean the house — up
and down, inside and out."

Sis gave each child a job. "Ben, you
mop. Take this bucket. Dot, you help
Bob make the beds. Wait until Mom
and Pop see this spotless home!"

Sis swept the halls. Ned dusted.
Todd scrubbed the windows.

At last the house was clean.

"Good work, kids!" said Sis. "Mom and Pop will be proud."

Then Sis gave them hugs.

Sis, Ben, Dot, Bob, Ned, and Todd slept well. They dreamed sweet dreams. They did not know what Dot forgot. Dot forgot to close the windows!

"Such a mess!" said Sis.
"What will Mom and Pop say?"

"Look!" said Bob. "It's Mom and Pop!"
"Surprise! Surprise!
We cleaned the house, Mom and Pop!
This mess is a surprise to us!"

Word Lists

Len and Linda's Picnic **(p. 1)** accompanies *Dragon Gets By.*

DECODABLE WORDS

Target Skill
Short Vowels *a, i*
am, an, at, ball, basket, big, can, catch, chin, did, drip, glad, hand, has, his, it, jam, Linda, Linda's, list, napkins, packed, pad, pal, picnic, plastic, ring, sad, sadly, sat, things, think, this, visit, will, window, with

Words Using Previously Taught Skills
be, bell, best, big, but, came, cloth, cups, day, den, drops, fun, game, get, glee, got, just, left, Len, luck, made, make, need, new, no, pen, plates, rain, raining, steps, stops, tea, them, then, toast, took, up, went, wet, when, yelled

HIGH-FREQUENCY WORDS

New
bought, front, kitchen, roll, until

Previously Taught
a, and, are, come, door, down, falling, found, he, her, I, in, is, indoor, jumped, know, look, looked, my, not, of, on, outside, play, said, see, she, soon, started, someone, the, thought, to, we, what, you

48

An Ice Cream Crash (p. 9) accompanies *Dragon Gets By.*

Target Skill (Review)
Word Endings *–s,–ed, –ing*
added, asked, bumped, crashing, ended, feeling, handed, helped, reached, rushed, scratched, twins, yelled

Words Using Previously Taught Skills
an, as, at, back, bad, bike, Bob's, boom, bump, but, can, cone, crash, cream, cry, each, fast, feel, food, from, fun, get, help, high, hill, his, home, ice, it, Jill, knee, let's, low, make, maybe, no, please, ride, Sam, steep, stop, store, that, then, this, took, town, trip, truck, twin, up, us, went, Will, zoom

Previously Taught
a, and, better, could, down, eating, for, going, hard, he, hungry, in, into, is, jumped, kitchen, looked, looking, my, not, of, on, other, rolled, said, started, starting, the, their, they, to, too, until, we, were, what, you

Big Hog's House Hunt (p. 17) accompanies *Julius.*

DECODABLE WORDS

Target Skill
Short Vowels *o, u, e*
bet, bus, but, cub, cub's, den, dog, extra, fun, gets, help, hog, hop, hopped, hot, hugged, hunt, job, just, led, let, let's, lot, lots, met, much, mud, pen, problem, sell, set, stop, such, sudden, sun, up, vet, web, welcome, went, when, yet

Words Using Previously Taught Skills
at, be, big, can, dark, fine, grand, happens, home, homes, it, keep, make, might, new, no, pals, road, sale, space, such, take, that, think, this, time, visit, will, yes

HIGH-FREQUENCY WORDS

New
brought, reason, special, surprise

Previously Taught
a, all, and, any, do, does, down, enough, five, for, found, give, good, have, he, here, house, I, is, it's, like, look, looking, me, more, my, near, of, off, or, present, right, said, see, so, the, to, too, was, we'll, you

50

Robin's Farm (p. 25) accompanies *Julius.*

Target Skill (Review)
Short Vowels *a*, *i*
Agnes, at, basket, big, brand, brings, cat, catches, chicks, Flash, grass, had, has, his, it, Jazz, milking, naps, pals, pickup, pig, piglets, pigs, pink, rabbit, rabbit's, Robin, Robin's, sat, sits, six, sticks, stand, this, will, window, with

Words Using Previously Taught Skills
barn, birth, closes, day, dog, ears, eggs, farm, feed, food, fur, gave, get, graze, hen, hops, hutch, large, late, mice, named, new, night, red, ride, rides, sleep, smiles, spot, spring, stay, store, striped, takes, then, truck, up, when, white, York

New
special, surprise

Previously Taught
a, about, and, animals, babies, brown, care, cows, door, for, go, good, green, he, her, head, horses, house, in, inside, is, live, many, now, of, or, on, out, play, she, the, they, three, to, warm

Jane's Mistake (p. 33) accompanies *Mrs. Brown Went to Town.*

DECODABLE WORDS

Target Skill
Long Vowels *a, i* (CVC*e*)
Ace, bracelet, came, chase, Crane, face, Fine, gave, hide, Jake, Jane, Jane's, Kate, Kate's, made, mine, mistake, name, nice, Race, take, smile

Words Using Previously Taught Skills
ask, at, be, bead, beads, big, but, did, each, Enjan, fast, from, gym, had, hall, has, held, if, it, just, kids, let's, might, Miss, missing, must, quick, red, Renna, spell, spelled, stopped, switch, thanks, that's, them, then, thing, think, this, took, went, will, with, yelled

HIGH-FREQUENCY WORDS

New
different, floor, letter, move, poor, word

Previously Taught
a, and, always, also, arm, began, don't, for, found, friends, her, I, in, inside, is, kind, letters, like, look, more, my, not, now, on, or, out, read, said, she, shout, someone, the, they, to, try, turn, we, wearing, who, whoever, you, your

The Big Surprise (p. 41*)* accompanies *Mrs. Brown Went to Town.*

Target Skill (Review)
Short Vowels *o, u, e*
beds, Ben, Bob, bucket, Dot, dusted, forgot, fun, help, hugs, job, let's, mess, Mom, mop, Ned, Pop, red, scrubbed, slept, spotless, such, swept, then, Todd, up, us, well, went

Words Using Previously Taught Skills
at, be, big, can, clean, cleaned, close, day, did, dreamed, dreams, each, fine, gave, halls, home, it's, kids, Lane, last, made, make, proud, red, say, Sis, six, sweet, take, them, this, trip, wait, will, windows

Previously Taught
a, and, children, down, good, have, house, in, inside, is, know, live, look, not, on, one, out, said, see, soon, surprise, the, they, to, too, until, was, we, what, work, you

HIGH-FREQUENCY WORDS TAUGHT TO DATE:

Grade 1	build	far	horse	ocean	second	try	Grade 2
a	butter	father	house	of	see	turn	bought
able	buy	find	how	off	seven	two	brought
about	by	first	hungry	old	shall	under	different
above	call	five	hurt	on	sharp	upon	floor
afraid	car	flower	I	once	she	very	front
after	carry	fly	idea	one	shoe(s)	walk	kitchen
again	caught	follow	in	only	shout	wall	letter
against	children	for	is	open	show	want	move
all	cling	forest	jump	or	sing	warm	poor
already	cold	found	kind	other	small	was	reason
also	color	four	know	our	so	wash	roll
always	come	friend	laugh	out	some	watched	special
and	could	full	learn	over	soon	water	surprise
animal	cow	funny	light	own	start	we	until
any	dance	garden	like	paper	sure	wear	word
are	divide	girl	little	part	table	were	
arms	do	give	live	people	talk	what	
around	does	go	long	person	tall	where	
away	done	goes	look	picture	teacher	who	
baby	door	gone	love	piece	the	why	
bear	down	good	many	play	their	work	
because	draw	green	me	present	there	world	
been	eat	grow	minute	pretty	these	would	
before	edge	happy	more	pull	they	write	
began	eight	hard	morning	put	thought	you	
begin	else	have	most	read	three	your	
bird	enough	he	mother	ready	through		
blue	evening	head	my	right	tiny		
body	ever	hear	near	room	to		
both	every	her	never	said	today		
break	fall	here	not	saw	together		
brown	family	hold	now	school	too		

Decoding Skills Taught to Date: Short Vowels *a, i;* Base Words and Endings *–s, -ed, -ing;* Short Vowels *o, u, e;* Structural Analysis: VCCV Pattern; Long Vowels *a, i* (CVC*e*)